From the Library of Jane Stubbs

Have you ever uncovered a hidden treasure of a book while browsing in some forgotten corner of a bookstore? I happened across *How to Behave and Why* in this fashion. Initially I was delighted by its bold red-and-black cover design, so simple and yet so arresting, and its charming stick-figure illustrations. It wasn't until I had read the book that I discovered its most enchanting feature: This book doesn't teach the most recent or fashionable etiquette of the day; it encourages a spirit of cooperation among people and a humanity that applies to societies the world over. This lesson is classic and timeless. I hope *How to Behave and Why* enchants you as it enchants me.

Your Name Here

HOW
TO
BEHAVE
AND
WHY

Damax noted
7/14/16 sfi per HW

Published by arrangement with HarperCollins Children's Books,
a Division of HarperCollins Publishers Inc.

Published in hardcover in the United States of America in 2002
by UNIVERSE PUBLISHING
A Division of Rizzoli International Publications, Inc.
300 Park Avenue South
New York, NY 10010
www.rizzoliusa.com

2012 2013 2014 / 23 22 21 20

Printed in China

ISBN-10: 0-7893-0684-0

ISBN-13: 978-0-7893-0684-5

Library of Congress Control Number: 2002100576

Cover desgn: Paul Kepple / Headcase Design
Universe editor: Jessica Fuller

HOW TO BEHAVE AND WHY

Munro Leaf

UNIVERSE

This

is really a book about how to have the most fun in living, and it doesn't matter whether you are a boy or a girl, a man or a woman — the rules are all the same.

How old we are isn't what counts.
The two biggest questions to ask
ourselves in life, at any age, are:

Are most of the people I know

glad that I am here?

Am I glad that I am here, myself?

Anyone who can honestly answer

"YES"

to those two questions most of

the time has learned to

BEHAVE

in this world and to live a

happy life.

It doesn't matter whether you are a

Chinese grandfather, an

Eskimo mother or an American boy

or girl going to school —

You still have to get along well with

other people and have

most of them like you, if you want

to be happy.

9

Ever since the days when men

stopped living in caves, the

good and decent people of the world

have found out that there

are certain ways we all have to be-

have if we want to live

together pleasantly.

The good ways, or the good rules

for behaving, have lasted a

long time — so they must have

something.

No matter where you are or who
you are, there are four
main things that you have to do if
you want to make good
friends and keep them.

You have to be HONEST

You have to be FAIR

You have to be STRONG

and

You have to be WISE

And there is no good

in trying

to fool yourself.

All that isn't so easy.

HONEST

FAIR

STRONG

WISE

Those are the four things you

have to be

SO

Let's take them apart slowly

and find out

— WHY?

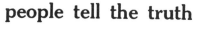

Honest

people tell the truth

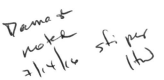

Other people know that when

<u>they</u> say something is so, they

can believe it.

Now that is very handy, because

15

if you are honest and promise to do something,

others will trust you.

They will share things with you,

tell you secrets,

lend you money,

and help you do many of

the things you want to do —

because

They know that what you promise

and what you say

is true.

They can count on it.

**O**nly

a dope will tell a lie.

One of the quickest ways to lose

your friends and to make people

dislike you is to lie.

Some people think they can be smart and fool

others when they tell a lie — but

sooner or later the truth usually is found out

and then the liar is sorry because

 he knows he won't be trusted

or believed the next time.

This one says his baby sister

broke that mirror.

Would you trust him

and want him for a friend?

No b o d y

knows what to do with a

person who doesn't tell the truth.

How can you believe a word they

say?

Even if they do tell the truth part of

the time, how can you know which

times they mean it

and

which times they don't?

No — we can't say that just one little

lie doesn't count.

It counts every time and people can't

really know us and like us unless they

can believe what we say.

E very

time we tell a lie we mix ourselves

up more.

After a while almost no one will believe us —

but worse than that —

We can't believe ourselves

or anyone else, because

we don't really

know <u>what</u>

<u>the truth is</u>

any more than a penguin

and that is a stupid way to live

As anyone can tell you.

Stealing

is something honest people don't do.

Taking things

that don't belong

to you is a sure way to get

into trouble and be unhappy.

Good people can't let bad people take things

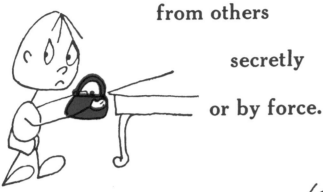

from others

secretly

or by force.

If they did

the world would be

a miserable place for everyone. Nothing we

own would be safe.

Grownups who steal are put in jail

in almost every country—

and that is one way a

person loses all his friends

for a long long time.

**T**here

is another way to make

people dislike you that is

half like lying and half

like stealing — and it's

just as bad as either of them.

That is

CHEATING.

In playing games

working at school

trading things or buying
or selling
the person
who cheats will make enemies
of those he cheats and

other people won't like or trust him.
Nothing we get by cheating
is worth what we lose
with our friends.

We have spelled out

HONEST

and all we have to do now

is to remember that

being HONEST is

probably the most important

rule of living a happy life.

In a way everything else we do

depends on it.

If we aren't honest, we really aren't

ourselves to others, and if we aren't ourselves

we certainly can't make friends and

 be happy.

YOU HAVE TO BE

FAIR

Friendly

people find it easy to be

FAIR.

Being friendly and being fair both come from

believing that other people have just as

much right to be alive and happy as we have.

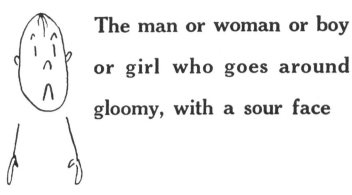

The man or woman or boy or girl who goes around gloomy, with a sour face

and is afraid that everybody else is going to make him or her unhappy has a very hard time making friends.

There are a lot of nice people everywhere and the sooner we meet each other in a friendly way and get to know each other, the better the world will be for all of us.

Anywhere

you go with a smile and a wish to like people, you

will find someone who will be glad to see you.

From Africa to the
Arctic Circle this is so.
People everywhere are
like yourself in many
ways and most of them
want to share happiness
and the good things of
life with others if you
will do the same.

SO —

Get up in the morning wherever you are and

go to school

or

play

or work

or parties

or new places

glad to meet new people and make old friends of them.

n

your own home is a good

place to begin every day

by being fair.

 Our mothers and fathers and sisters

and brothers make wonderful friends,

if we treat them fairly and do our

share to make home a happy place

for everyone there.

Helping to keep it neat and clean.

Sharing the work that has to be done.

Being quiet when others need peace.

And giving others just as much right as you
have to enjoy themselves with or without you —
There are all ways of being Fair and ways
to make people glad you live with them from
the time you wake in the morning until you
pleasantly, cheerfully go to bed.

R emember

the secret of fairness is sharing.

Selfish people who won't share with others find

themselves left alone and unhappy no matter

what they own that

could be fun.

Look out for the person who pretends to be
your friend

but doesn't want you to like anyone else. That
isn't a friend — it's a selfish person who is trying to own you and hasn't learned to share
to be happy.

Poor sports who can't lose
games without squawk-
ing or won't take turns
are not FAIR

and

Neither is the lazy lump
who never shares
the work that has
to be done by
someone.

We know now what it means to be FAIR

and we will learn all through life that the friendly person is a happy person most of the time.

YOU HAVE TO BE

STRONG

Some

people think that being strong

is just a matter of having

muscles like a gorilla.

But they are wrong.

That alone never made anybody

happy

Real strength comes from having

a clean, healthy mind and

a clean, healthy body.

T h i n k

it out for yourself.
All the power of sixty gorillas won't do you
any good if you use it stupidly, and if you don't
stay healthy you might as well be a run down

mouse.

Any brave man or woman can tell you that having a clean healthy mind comes from taking the time to think what is right and then doing it

no matter

how scared you are

or

when it would be easier to do wrong

or

even if somebody else tries to talk you into it.

Regular

habits are the answer to the question:

How can we grow from a weak baby

to a strong and healthy man or woman?

Eating the right food
when we should

Keeping clean

Playing and exercising

Sitting and standing right
and

getting the right amount of
sleep and rest are

HOW TO GROW WELL
AND STRONG

Of

course you can argue

with people who know better than you, but

it's stupid.

Doctors and scientists study and

learn what is the best way to keep

ourselves healthy.

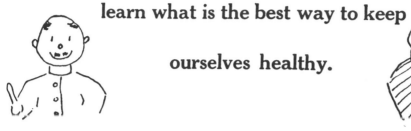

Our fathers and mothers

learn from them and they

tell us.

They know a lot more than we

do, and if we are bright, we do

what they tell us to.

**N** o w

is the best time

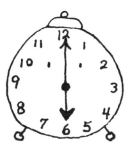

to start doing what you are told to do

for your own good health.

You can ask your parents to tell you

WHY

they want you to obey,

BUT

Don't Nag

and

Whine

and

Grumble

and

Cry

every time you just don't want to do

what is right.

Grown ups

aren't some kind

of weird monsters

that have fun

making us

do things

we don't want

to do.

They just know a

whole lot more than we do

because they have been here longer.

Listen

to what they tell you

and you will be surprised how right

they usually are.

We all are different in many ways,

but

we are all alike in many ways too.

If we are

HONEST

and

FAIR

and

STRONG

We won't find it hard to be wise.

YOU HAVE TO BE

WISE

We

get along with people and we make good friends

when we have polite manners like:

Shaking hands when we meet.

★ ★

Smiling and saying "good morning" or "good afternoon"

★ ★

Saying "goodbye" when we leave and thanking people when

they have been nice to us.

Saying "Please" when we want something and "Excuse me" or "I beg your pardon," when we bump into someone, or belch or yawn or cough or sneeze. (And when we yawn or cough we cover our mouths.)

★　★

Waiting for other people to finish talking before we start.

★　★

Letting ladies and girls be "first."

★　★

Helping very old and very young people as much as we can, and being quiet and gentle when we are with them.

★　★

Eating quietly without sprawling and grabbing or quarreling at the table. Asking to be excused when we have finished eating and are ready to leave.

★　★

Being quiet and orderly when we go to places where there are a lot of other people — like libraries, movies or museums, theatres or classrooms, or in trains, street cars or busses.

★　★

By never acting as though we were the only people in the world who counted, and never acting fresh and showing off to make people believe that we think we are better than they are.

"I can't always be right

no matter who

I am"

is a good thing for all

of us to remember.

Other people have ideas and thoughts

ways to do things

ways to work

ways to play

ways they think of God

and

their country

and

their race.

Their way can be just as right

as

your way.

Remember that, and be glad you

have a chance to choose

the best of all ways.

S ailing

together in a boat is a lot like learn-

ing to live with other people and be

happy.

We learn to obey and

after a while we

learn to command

and help to make

the world a

better place

for

all of us.

E n d

of the book is

what this is,

and if

YOU

learned

to be

HONEST

★

FAIR

★

STRONG

★

WISE

★

Then you have learned

HOW
TO
BEHAVE--
AND WHY